Arnt Cobbers (Text)
Günter Schneider (Photos

New Architecture in Berlin

Jaron Verlag

HISTORISCHES

New Berlin

Almost two decades have passed since Berlin was reunified. And it has been almost two decades of ongoing construction. The appearance of the city has changed a lot, in some places quite drastically. Architecturally Berlin is a different city than it was at the end of the 1980s. It is true that some hopes and expectations were not fulfilled. Some sites leave you wondering if it couldn't have been done better. But there is much to admire and enjoy among the buildings erected in re-unified Berlin. This book presents a small but representative selection from the city's central areas. It is organized geographically beginning at the Spree-bogen and continues clockwise. Brief information about the architect and year of completion is also provided.
It is far too early to make a final judgment. Berlin is, after all, still undergoing transformation. The speed of change has slowed down a bit, but if you walk through the city with open eyes, you'll notice an extraordinary number of construction cranes and buildings under scaffolding. Completely new neighborhoods are being created around the Hauptbahnhof, Berlin's new main train station, and at Osthafen. It is still very exciting and there is much to discover in "New Berlin".

Spreebogen

Reichstag Building
(Plenary Hall and Cupola)
Platz der Republik, Tiergarten
Norman Foster (London)
1995–1999

Paul Löbe Building
Konrad-Adenauer-Strasse 1,
Tiergarten
Stephan Braunfels
(Munich)
1997–2002

The **Reichstag Building** has served as the seat of the Bundestag, the German Parliament, since 1999. The London architect Sir Norman Foster completely redesigned the interior of this neo-Renaissance structure and replaced the old steel and glass cupola with a new glass dome that hovers above the plenary hall at the building's center. Natural light is directed into the plenary hall through a cleverly-designed system of reflectors. A ramp winds leisurely up the dome, offering visitors a lovely view of the city. — The Paul Löbe Building, which is connected to the Reichstag by an underground passageway, houses most of the conference rooms of the special committees and parliamentary parties. The **Federal Chancellery**, the power center of German politics, is right across the street.

Federal Chancellery
Willy-Brandt-Strasse 1, Tiergarten
Axel Schultes and Charlotte Frank (Berlin)
1997–2001

Marie Elisabeth Lüders
Building
Schiffbauerdamm/
Wilhelmstrasse, Mitte
Stephan Braunfels (Munich)
1998–2003

Federal Ribbon

The area called the **Federal Ribbon** cuts right across the Spreebogen, the bend in the Spree, and ends on the west side at the Chancellery Gardens. The head of state's home is shaped like an "H" with offices grouped around glassed-in courtyards in the side wings. The chancellor's office and the federal cabinet conference room are located at the center of the upper levels of the 36-meter high "main building." – The two parliamentary structures, the **Paul Löbe Building** and the **Marie Elisabeth Lüders Building,** look rather clunky from above, but seen from the ground, they appear more delicate than the Chancellery building. They are connected across the Spree by two overlapping bridges – one public, the other for internal use.

Paul Löbe Building

Swiss Embassy
Otto-von-Bismarck-Allee 5,
Tiergarten
Diener + Diener (Basel)
1999–2000

The **Swiss Embassy** is the only surviving pre-war building on the Spreebogen. A minimalist concrete cube structure was added to the neo-Classical building. — The federal president resides in the classical Bellevue Palace and his administration works in the **President's Office**, a new building next door which was given the popular nick-name "president's egg" in reference to its unusual form. The entire staff has a view of the palace grounds from their offices. The secondary rooms, stairwells and elevators, are concentrated in a rectangular wing at the center of the building which is encircled by a glass atrium. — The so-called **Federal Snake** refers to a 320-meter long winding structure with 700 apartments originally built as federal employee housing.

Federal Snake
Apartment
Complex
Joachim-Karnatz-
Allee 1-43,
Tiergarten
Georg Bumiller
(Berlin)
1996–1999

resident's Office
preeweg 1,
iergarten
lartin Gruber,
elmut Kleine-
raneburg
Frankfurt/Main)
996–1998

DB

For now the **Hauptbahnhof**, Berlin's new main train station, stands alone in the middle of nowhere at the historic site of the Lehrter Station. It is the city's first major junction station: East-west traffic intersects the city above the street level on the city rail embankment. Trains depart from the station's long glass hall. The track platforms for trains traveling north and south lie underground and a new tunnel allows traffic to cross beneath the Spree and Tiergarten. — The **Hamburger Bahnhof** has served as a museum for contemporary art since 1996. The terminal station first opened in 1847. After World War II it was East German property, but situated in West Berlin and hence left to decay. Josef Paul Kleihues successfully converted it into an attractive exhibition space.

Hauptbahnhof
Invalidenstrasse,
Tiergarten
gmp von Gerkan
Marg & Partner
(Hamburg)
1995–2006

amburger Bahnhof Museum
vith alterations and addition)
ıvalidenstrasse 50/51,
'ergarten
ısef Paul Kleihues (Berlin)
ı90–1995

Press and Information Office
of the Federal Government
Reichstagufer/Neustädtische
Kirchstrasse, Mitte
KSP Engel und Zimmermann
(Braunschweig)
1996–2000

ARD-Capital Studio
Reichstagufer 7-8/
Wilhelmstrasse, Mitte
Manfred and Laurids Ortner
(Vienna)
1996–1999

Federal Press Conference
Schiffbauerdamm 40, Mitte
Johanne and Gernot Nalbach
(Berlin)
1998–2000

Most of the major media offices are located close to the parliament building. The **Federal Press Conference** is an independent association of political journalists. Important and powerful figures of German national politics appear regularly before the press in the large conference hall at the center of the building. At night the building on the bank of the Spree is dramatically illuminated. — The weekly television news program “Bericht aus Berlin” broadcasts from the the capital studio of First German Television (ARD) in a severe geometrical concrete building on the Spree. The different window formats reflect each level’s different function. A large atrium forms the heart of the structure. — The **Federal Government’s Press and Information Office** consists of a complex of older buildings.

Mitte-Nord

The Charité, Berlin's largest hospital, forms its own city within the city and contains a few interesting new structures tucked between the many neo-Gothic brick buildings. The **Max Planck Institute for Infection Biology**, for example, has a very unusual sculptural entrance front. — There are also a few federal ministries situated in the Friedrich-Wilhelm-Stadt. The **Ministry for Research and Education** moved into what had been the "Permanent Diplomatic Office of the Federal Republic of Germany" in the Capital of the GDR. The ministry office is located in a narrow elevated annex that juts out from the western side of the building. The bright red walls, box-shaped projection and glass bay windows beneath it create a strong contrast to the otherwise practically-designed structure. — The extension added to the **Building and Transport Ministry**, a cube with a courtyard, displays an unrelenting, severe grid façade.

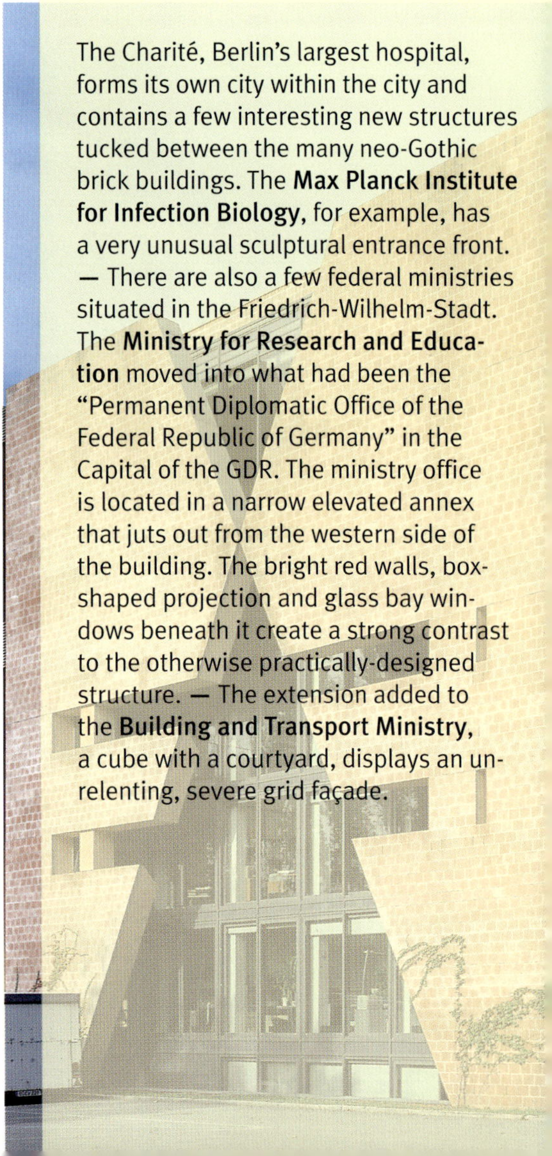

Federal Ministry for
Education and Research
(remodeled with new addition)
Hannoversche Strasse 30,
Mitte
Jourdan & Müller
(Frankfurt/Main)
1999–2000

Max Planck Institute
for Infection Biology
Charité, Schumann-
strasse 20-21, Mitte
Hannelore Deubzer,
Jürgen König (Berlin)
1997–1999

Federal Ministry for
Building and Transport
(new addition)
Invalidenstrasse 44,
Mitte
Max Dudler (Berlin)
1997–1999

26 qm Laden

Chapel of Reconciliation
Bernauer Strasse 4, Wedding
reitermann/sassenroth
Architekten (Berlin)
1999–2000

An unusual structure on Bernauer Strasse was dedicated in 2000. After 1961 the neo-Gothic Reconciliation Church that once stood here found itself on the border strip behind the Berlin Wall. It was torn down in 1985. The **Chapel of Reconciliation**, erected in its place, is oval shaped with an outer wall made of pounded clay encircled by a dense exterior of wooden beams. — The most unusual residential buildings in Mitte were often built to fill empty lots or close off a corner. The narrow building on Hessische Strasse is called **Bender** and looks from the front like it has been cut into three parts: One third of the façade is completely glass. The other two sections are wrapped in steel "bands" that run along the entire building.

'Bender" residential building
Hessische Strasse 5,
Mitte
deadline (Matthew Griffin
and Britta Jürgens, Berlin)
2003–2004

Pariser Platz

Hotel Adlon
Unter den Linden 75-77, Mitte
Patzschke, Klotz & Partner (Berlin)
1995–1997

A glaring contrast: The architects of the newly constructed **Hotel Adlon** returned to the basic form and architectural language of the original luxury hotel that was destroyed in the war, but they added an additional level while maintaining the height of the original building. Consequently, the new interior utterly lacks the spaciousness of the pre-war building. — The new **Academy of Arts** building, located at the original site of its predecessor, exempted itself from the requirement that all buildings on the plaza be made fifty percent of stone. A glass roof on the inside protects the preserved original 1905/06 atelier and exhibition rooms. — The **DZ-Bank** conceals a fancifully-shaped glass and metal construction in its interior courtyard – by far the most unusual conference hall in the city.

DZ-Bank
Pariser Platz 3, Mitte
Frank O. Gehry (Santa Monica)
1997–2000

Academy of Arts
Pariser Platz 4, Mitte
Günter Behnisch, Manfred Sabatke (Stuttgart)
2000–2004

American Embassy
Pariser Platz 2, Mitte
Moore Ruble Yudell
(Santa Monica)
2004–08

The United States took its time building a new structure for its Berlin residence. The **American Embassy** next the Brandenburg Gate did not officially open until 2008. Construction was delayed because of years of disputes with the Berlin Senate over security issues. In the end the city agreed to shift the position of Behrenstrasse, which runs south, over a bit, but it refused to block off part of Pariser Platz to pedestrians as the U.S. had wanted. The vehicle barriers surrounding the new building suggest that post-nine-eleven security concerns had a major influence on the building plans. Architecture critics were unanimous in their rejection of the design. The Palais Blücher stood at this site from 1939 to 1941 and was used by the Americans as an embassy.

Dresdner Bank's
Eugen Gutmann House
Pariser Platz 5a-6, Mitte
gmp von Gerkan Marg & Partner
(Hamburg)
1996–1997

The new **Embassies of France** and **Great Britain** were also erected at the sites where their previous embassies had stood before the war. Although the French Embassy's façade adheres strictly to the design regulations for Pariser Platz, it still succeeds in standing out. The unusual positioning of the windows conceals the interior structure of the building. The British architect Michael Wilford got around the idea of a "Berlin of stone" by having colorful structural elements protrude onto the street from an otherwise dull façade of holes. — In contrast, the Dresdner Bank's **Eugen Gutmann House** has an austere exterior structure with the window pairs, roof and high portal lending a touch of humor to the façade.

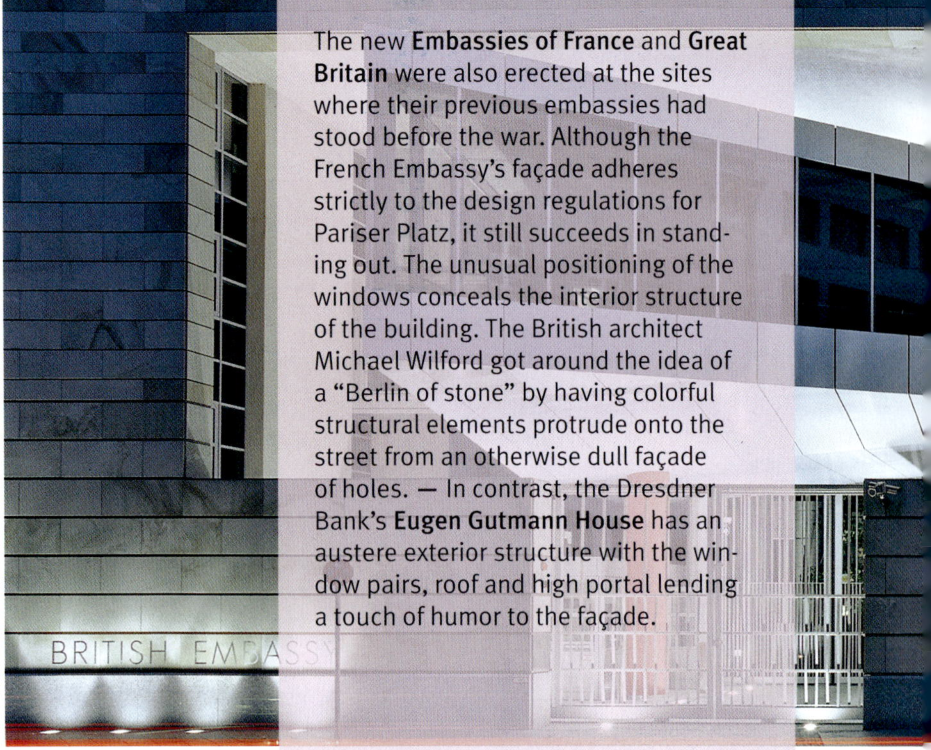

British Embassy
Wilhelmstrasse 70-71, Mitte
Michael Wilford (London)
1998–2000

French Embassy
Pariser Platz 5, Mitte
hristian de Portzamparc
(Paris)
1999–2002

Ministerial Gardens

South of the Brandenburg Gate, a large field of steles commemorates the European Jews who died in the Holocaust. The 2700 concrete columns are set on an undulating foundation and graduated in height to create a poignant relief. They are 15 centimeters wide and hollow and each has a basic size of 2.4 by .95 meters. The tallest ones measure 4.7 meters. There are 95-centimeter wide paths set between them. Commenting on his design, Peter Eisenman, the architect of the **Holocaust Memorial**, said: “The enormity and horror of the Holocaust is such that any attempt to represent it by traditional means is inevitably inadequate. (...) Our memorial attempts to present a new idea of memory as distinct from nostalgia.” An underground “Site of Information” is connected to the memorial.

Memorial for the Murdered Jews of Europe
Behrenstrasse/Ebertstrasse, Mitte
Peter Eisenman (New York)
2003–2005

Hesse State Representation Office
In den Ministergärten 5, Mitte
Michael Christl, Joachim Bruchhäuser (Frankfurt/Main)
1999–2000

Lower Saxony and Schleswig-Holstein State Representation Offices
In den Ministergärten 8-19, Mitte
Cornelsen & Seelinger/ Seelinger & Vogels (Amsterdam/Darmstadt)
1999–2000

Federal State Representation Offices in the Ministerial Gardens

Saarland State
Representation Office
In den Ministergärten 4,
Mitte
Alt & Britz (Saarbrücken)
1999–2000

The international embassies are often outdone by the architecture of the German federal states' representation offices in the capital. Five new buildings representing seven federal states were erected on the grounds of the former Ministerial Gardens. The state offices of **Lower Saxony** and **Schleswig-Holstein** share a building, as do **Brandenburg** and **Mecklenburg-Vorpommern**. The aerial photo reveals how the building wings are separated by glass atriums (above left and below right). The building block containing the two northern federal state offices is enlivened by red metal profiles and the irregular placement of windows. The cube-shaped structure representing the state of **Saarland** opens up into a grid at the rear. The **Hesse** state office displays an unusual vibrancy. Thanks to protruding levels and the accentuation of the horizontal, it is the most striking of the buildings in the Ministerial Gardens.

Potsdamer and Leipziger Platz

War and the division of the city left behind a huge wasteland at Potsdamer Platz and the neighboring Leipziger Platz. One of the largest building projects of new Berlin entailed creating a new city district to fill this emptiness. By 2005, many office, business, hotel and residential structures were finished in the Daimler, Sony and Beisheim quarters – with very different architecture. To the surprise of many critics, the concept works: Thanks to flourishing businesses, cinemas and theaters, the quarter is packed with tourists and locals both day and night. The most spectacular building is the **Sony Center**, a high-tech complex of steel and glass. The Forum opens on many sides and is covered by a magnificent tent-like roof structure.

Sony Center
Potsdamer/Bellevue-/
Ben-Gurion-Strasse,
Tiergarten
Helmut Jahn (Chicago)
1996–1999

Office Building at Potsdamer Platz 1, Tiergarten
Hans Kollhoff, Helga Timmermann (Berlin)
1997–2000

Office Building at Potsdamer Platz 11, Tiergarten
Renzo Piano (Paris),
Christoph Kohlbecker (Gaggenau)
1995–1998

Sony Center

Beisheim Center
Potsdamer Strasse/Ebertstrasse/
Lennéstrasse, Tiergarten
various architects
2001–2003

The quarter situated southwest of Potsdamer Platz is characterized by many different colored façades of stone, terracotta and ceramic plates. The **Debis Building**, crowned by a green cube resting 85-meters above ground, is a landmark seen from quite a distance. — The three **residential and office buildings** created by the star architect Richard Rogers are an eye-catcher. — David Chipperfield designed the luxury **Parkside Apartments** on the southern edge of the Tiergarten. — The **Beisheim Center** north of Potsdamer Platz is distinguished by its severe façades of varying materials. — The exterior of the Ritz Carlton, located right on Potsdamer Platz, emits stylish reserve while the interior wallows in plush and pomp. — In contrast, the lobby of the **Grand Hyatt** exhibits cool elegance.

Debis Building
Marlene-Dietrich-Platz 3-5, Tiergarten
Renzo Piano, Christoph Kohlbecker
1994–97

Parkside Apartments
Am Park, Tiergarten
David Chipperfield
(London)
2002–2003

Hotel Grand Hyatt
Marlene-Dietrich-Platz 2,
Tiergarten
José Rafael Moneo (Madrid)
1995–1998

Apartment and Office Building
Linkstrasse 6, Tiergarten
Richard Rogers (London)
1995–1998

Leipziger Plat
(in foreground

Office and Apartment Buildings
Leipziger Platz 10, Mitte
Axel Schultes (Berlin)
1999–2000

Mosse Palace
Leipziger Platz 15, Mitte
Hans Dieter Strauch, Schneider & Partner (Berlin)
1996–98

Potsdamer Platz is simply a large intersection but **Leipziger Platz** was designed as an octagon in the 1730s. It was named in 1814 after Prussia's victorious "Battle of the Nations" near Leipzig. The new architecture restores the original plaza structure. All the new buildings (with businesses, offices and apartments on the upper levels) have ten or eleven stories but beginning at the eighth floor they are set back from the front. Design regulations did not allow entirely glass fronts. Before it was destroyed during and after World War II, the Wertheim department store was the most prominent building on the plaza (located on the northeast side facing Leipziger and Voßstrasse). The future of these large grounds still remains open.

Downtown Mitte

Quartier 206
Friedrichstrasse 71-74,
Mitte
Henry Cobb (New York)
1992–1996

A large number of new businesses and department stores oriented mostly toward upper-class customers have opened on Friedrichstrasse. The Friedrichstadtpassagen is a true shopping paradise: the three blocks known as “Quartiere” in the baroque Friedrichstadt are connected by an underground passageway. The Berlin branch of the famous Paris department store **Galeries Lafayette** has a dark glass façade that is divided by horizontal metal bands. At the center of the building the inner courtyard is replaced by two plexiglass cones resting on each other. In contrast, the neighboring building, **Quartier 206**, is saturated in jagged art deco forms and elegant materials. The expressive exterior is also dramatically illuminated by night.

Galeries Lafayette
Friedrichstrasse 75,
Mitte
Jean Nouvel (Paris)
1993–1996

Townhouses on
Friedrichswerder
between Kurstrasse and
Ober-/Niederwallstrasse
Bernd Albers, Johanne
and Gernot Nalbach,
Theo Brenner, Behles &
Jochimsen, Abcarius +
Burns
Begun in 2005

GSW Building
Kochstrasse 22a, Kreuzberg
Matthias Sauerbach,
Louisa Hutton
1995–1999

Foreign Office
(front building)
Werderscher Markt,
Mitte
Thomas Müller,
Ivan Reimann (Berlin)
1997–1999

Berlin has a different look here: Since 2005 forty-seven **Berlin Townhouses** have been built on the historic Friedrichswerder, east of Gendarmenmarkt. Most of the houses are 6.5 meters wide and five stories high. Ten basic designs by renowned architects were used as the models for creating the individual buildings. — Beyond the arm of the Spree lies the **Foreign Office** with its stately front building, a newly erected addition. Its compact cube shape has been cleverly interrupted by a glass atrium at the entrance and two glass-covered courtyards on the sides facing the Spree and older building. — The Central Administration of the **GSW Building** Company, one of the cities most colorful high-rises, comes into view to the south. The red blinds are designed to protect the offices from direct sunlight.

Pei Building (New wing of the German Historical Museum)
Hinter dem Gießhaus, Mitte
I.M. Pei (New York)
1998–2003

Over the last two decades a number of German cities treated themselves to new, large, prestigious museums built by famous architects. The Chinese-born architect I.M. Pei, who lives and works in the United States, was asked to design the addition to the **German Historical Museum** in Berlin – a choice that proved to be a stroke of luck. A glass spiral staircase draws pedestrians from the glorious Unter den Linden avenue around the baroque Zeughaus and into the new museum wing. Pei concentrated the exhibition rooms into a central almost windowless structure clad in natural stone and enclosed by a spacious glass foyer, which through wall openings, gallery levels and pillars, is cleverly intertwined with the central structure. The interior of the building offers an impressive play of light and shadow in the foyer.

One of the most successful new buildings of recent years was erected at Am Kupfergraben, between the Pei building and Museum Island: David Chipperfield created an angular structure for the **Bastians**, an art collector couple, to use as a **gallery** and private museum. The façades, built of old whitened bricks, have only a few large window openings — The famous architect Rem Koolhaas' design of the **Netherlands Embassy** is quite different. He placed a gauze-like exterior around an L-shaped structure that encloses a glass cube. — The "scaly" titanium-zinc façade which encases the steel and concrete structure near the Molkenmarkt resembles the skin of a fish. This image association is intentional: This is the headquarters of the **Berlin Waterworks Company**.

Gallery Bastian
Am Kupfergraben 10, Mitte
David Chipperfield/ Alexander Schwarz
2003–07

Berlin Waterworks Company
Stralauer Str. 32, Mitte
Christoph Langhof
1998–2000

Netherlands
Embassy
alauer Strasse
44-47, Mitte
Rem Koolhaas
(Rotterdam)
1997–2003

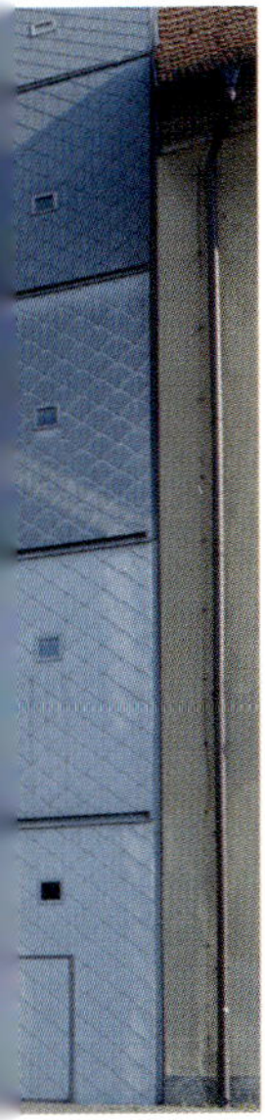

Radialsystem V
Holzmarktstrasse 33,
Friedrichshain
Gerhard Spangenberg
2004–06

Trias
Holzmarktstrasse 15-18,
Friedrichshain
Lucia Beringer, Günther
Wawrik (Munich)
1993–1996

The bank of the Spree to the east of the city center was overlooked for a long time. But recently new interesting architecture has emerged here and Berlin city planners have focused their attention on the area. The main headquarters of the Berlin Transportation System (BVG) occupies one of the first new buildings here. Three versions of the same structure were erected along the railroad tracks, which explains the fitting name **Trias**. — The **Radialsystem V** has become a popular location for concerts. The original brick building, built in 1905 and heavily damaged in World War II, had operated as the fifth pumping station of the Berlin waterworks. Gerhard Spangenberg expanded the building to include a glass addition that envelopes the top of the older structure on the Spree side.

RADIALSYSTEM

Kreuzberg

The northwest section of today's Kreuzberg district was established in the 18th century. The three-winged building which housed the superior court and now functions as the older building of the **Jewish Museum** is a relict from this period of urban expansion. It leads to the museum's new building, which, only accessible from underground, is probably the most widely acclaimed new architecture in Berlin. The Polish-born American Daniel Libeskind won the architectural competition to create an addition to the Berlin Museum. That was before the Berlin Wall fell in 1989 and before the "Berlin of stone" became the dominant image of a city amidst reunification. Libeskind erected an independent structure on an irregular, jagged ground plan. The zinc-clad exterior provides no clue to the interior space and floor layout. There are three upper exhibition floors and an office level beneath the flat roof.

Jewish Museum
Lindenstrasse 9-14,
Kreuzberg
Daniel Libeskind (Berlin)
1993–2001

An aerial view reveals a straight line cutting right through the building's east-west axis. The five intersecting spaces extend to the top of the building and can only be crossed with bridges. These voids symbolize the emptiness that remained in Berlin after the Jews were expelled and murdered. The "Holocaust Tower," a 24-meter high empty memorial space, stands adjacent to the building. — Kreuzberg, a working-class district, is a fitting location for the Social Democratic Party headquarters. The **Willy Brandt House** lies on a pie-shaped plot of land and its outline and detail call to mind a ship. The building-high glass atrium at the center is used for special events. The ground floor is filled with shops and a bistro.

Jewish Museum

lly Brandt House
Stresemann-
sse 28/Wilhelm-
rasse, Kreuzberg
Helge Bofinger
(Wiesbaden)
1993–1996

Berlin Galle
Alte Jakobstrasse 124-12
Kreuzbe
Kühn Malvezzi (Berli
2003–200

Over the last few years a number of large halls have been built in Berlin for sports, concerts and conventions. The most striking building is the **Tempodrom**, a 37-meter high tent construction made of reinforced concrete plates. Light flows into the hall, which holds 3,800 spectators, through a glass opening at the top. — Thirty years after its founding, the **Berlin Gallery**, the city's local museum of modern art, photography and architecture, finally found an ideal permanent location for its collection in a completely remodeled glass factory. — The **German Technology Museum's** new building lies where the Landwehr Canal, street, elevated rail and former railroad tracks intersect. A "Raisin Bomber," a veteran plane from the Allied Airlift of 1948/49, is suspended from its roof.

Tempodrom
Möckernstrasse 10-25,
Kreuzberg
gmp von Gerkan Marg
& Partner (Hamburg)
1999–2001

German Technology
Museum in Berlin
(new addition)
Trebbiner Strasse 9,
Kreuzberg
Ulrich Wolff, Helge Pitz
(Berlin)
1995–2003

Tiergarten/Diplomats Quarter

Austrian Embassy
Tiergartenstrasse 12-14,
Tiergarten
Hans Hollein (Vienna)
1999–2000

Mexican Embassy
Klingelhöferstrasse 3,
Tiergarten
Teodoro Gonzales de Léon,
Francisco Serrano
(Mexiko City)
1998–2000

Embassy of the United Arab Emirates
iroshimastrasse 16-20, Tiergarten
ause + Bohne (Aachen)
2002–2003

In the 1990s a number of new embassy buildings were erected in the old diplomat's quarter on the southern edge of the Tiergarten park. Many of the diplomatic buildings in Berlin, like the **Embassy of the United Arab Emirates**, which, surprisingly, was designed by a German architecture firm, make reference through their designs to their own country's unique local architecture. — The **Embassy of Mexico** has a captivating "classical modern" façade: Concrete slats hang on a concrete frame like lightly dispersed Venetian blinds. The entrance leads through the two concealed fronts to a central rotunda. — The **Austrian Embassy** is a little trendier: Its reception rooms are grouped around a central atrium in a green-clad structure. The offices are located in the long wing encased in natural stone. The ambassador's residence with its light red plaster front is nestled between the other two building sections.

Embassy of India
Tiergartenstrasse 16-17,
Tiergarten
Hilde Léon, Konrad Wohlhage,
Siegfried Wernik (Berlin)
1999–2001

The world's nations have clearly gotten caught up in the excitement of Berlin's construction boom. No other capital has so many high-quality embassy buildings. Norway, Sweden Denmark, Finland and Iceland united their diplomatic offices into a single complex. The five **Nordic embassies** and a shared "community house" ar linked by a curvilinear copper band that extends over the entire height o the building. — The Berlin architects who designed the **Indian Embassy** used a roughly cut sandstone from India for the façade. — The **CDU national party headquarters** is located close by on the Landwehr Canal on an acutely-angled piece of property. A rounded "body of a ship" is encased by a glassed-in winter garden.

CDU National
Party Head-
quarters
Klingelhöfer-
strasse 8,
Tiergarten
Petzinka,
ink & Partner
(Düsseldorf)
1999–2000

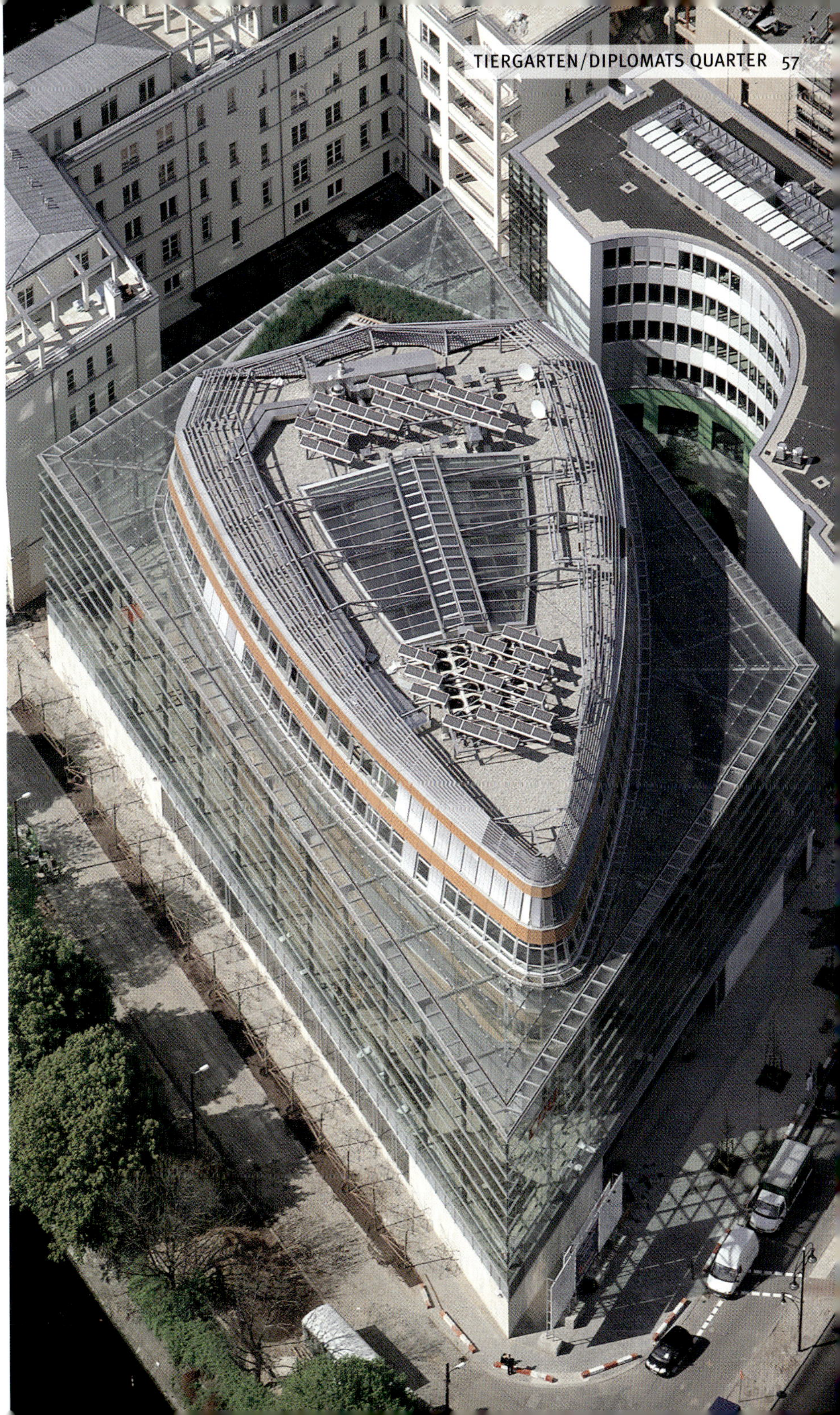

ordic
nbassies
uchstrasse 1,
ergarten
fred Berger,
na Parkkinen
ienna)
97–1999

City-West

New Kranzler-Eck
Kurfürstendamm/
Joachimsthaler Strasse,
Charlottenburg
Helmut Jahn (Chicago)
1998–2000

Swissôtel
(New Kudamm-Eck)
Kurfürstendamm 227-228,
Charlottenburg
gmp von Gerkan, Marg &
Partner (Hamburg)
2000–2001

Ludwig Erhard Building
Fasanenstrasse 83-84,
Charlottenburg
Nicholas Grimshaw
(London)
1994–1998

With each new year the Berlin Tourism Office registers new record numbers and consequently, a number of new hotels have been built. The **Swissôtel** logo has hovered above the intersection of Kurfürstendamm and Joachimsthaler Strasse since 2001. The Swiss hotel occupies the upper floors of the New Kudamm-Eck. A fashion department store moved into the lower levels. — Diagonally opposite, the **New Kranzler-Eck**, powerful and razor-sharp, juts out onto Kurfürstendamm from behind the older more traditional Kranzler-Eck. — The **Ludwig Erhard Building**, home to the Berlin Stock Exchange, takes its form from an armadillo. Unfortunately, the district building authority demanded that the façade remain evenly vertical all the way up to the eaves on the side facing Fasanenstrasse.

Sports Arenas

Olympic Stadium
(alteration)
Olympischer Platz,
Charlottenburg
gmp von Gerkan,
Marg & Partner
(Hamburg)
2002–2005

O2-World
Mühlenstrasse 12-30,
Friedrichshain
No architect listed.
2006–08

Velodrom
Landsberger Allee/
Paul-Heyse-Strasse,
Prenzlauer Berg
Dominique Perrault
(Paris)
1993–1996

Max-Schmeling-Halle
Am Falkplatz,
Prenzlauer Berg
Joppien Dietz
Architekten
(Frankfurt/Main)
1993–1997

Even though Berlin's offer to host the 2000 Olympic Summer Games was rejected, the **Olympic Stadium**, built for the 1936 Olympic Summer Games, was still completely renovated. It was a slippery slope between modernization and memorial preservation: The playing field was sunk into the ground, the lower level redone and the upper level and external construction were renovated according to memorial preservation requirements. The elegant roof construction which leaves only the marathon gate uncovered lends it the name "new" Olympic stadium. The stadium, situated on the vast Olympic grounds, is now used for concerts, major sports events and soccer games played by Hertha BSC, Berlin's national soccer team. — The **Velodrom** cycling coliseum is sunk into the earth and from the outside looks like a flat, shiny silver disc without a street front. — The main arena of the **Max-Schmeling-Halle** seats 10,000 people beneath its unusually voluminous roof. — But **O2-World** in Friedrichshain recently established itself as Berlin's largest sports and all-purpose stadium with space for up to 17,000 guests. More proof that big architecture does not always make for good architecture.

Index of Architects

The Author

Arnt Cobbers, born in the Lower Rhein region, has lived in Berlin since 1985. He received his doctorate in art history and history and works as a cultural affairs journalist and book author. He has written the texts for many successful photography books published by Jaron Verlag.

The Photographer

Günter Schneider, born in 1955, is one of the most successful Berlin photographers. Architectural and aerial photography are his areas of expertise. Many of his superb photography books of contemporary Berlin were published by Jaron Verlag. (www.guenterschneider.de)

Imprint

1st Edition 2009

(Original title: "Neue Architektur in Berlin")

www.jaron-verlag.de
Translation: Miriamne Fields, Berlin
Map: Matthias Frach, Berlin
Public transportation map: BVG
Cover design: Atelier Kattner, Berlin using photographs by Günter Schneider
Design and layout:
Prill Partners | producing, Berlin
Lithography: LVD GmbH, Berlin
Printed and bound by:
Westermann Druck Zwickau
ISBN 978-3-89773-611-5
ISBN 978-3-89773-612-2 (5 copies)